Unlocking the Secrets of Science

Profiling 20th Century Achievers in Science, Medicine, and Technology

Henry Ford and the Assembly Line

∙∙

John Bankston

Mitchell Lane
PUBLISHERS

PO Box 619 • Bear, Delaware 19701
www.mitchelllane.com

Unlocking the Secrets of Science

Profiling 20th Century Achievers in Science, Medicine, and Technology

Luis Alvarez and the Development of the Bubble Chamber
Marc Andreessen and the Development of the Web Browser
Oswald Avery and the Story of DNA
Frederick Banting and the Discovery of Insulin
Christiaan Barnard and the Story of the First Successful Heart Transplant
Tim Berners-Lee and the Development of the World Wide Web
Chester Carlson and the Development of Xerography
Wallace Carothers and the Story of DuPont Nylon
Francis Crick and James Watson: Pioneers in DNA Research
Jacques-Yves Cousteau: His Story Under the Sea
Raymond Damadian and the Development of the MRI
Gerhard Domagk and the Discovery of Sulfa
Paul Ehrlich and Modern Drug Development
Albert Einstein and the Theory of Relativity
Willem Einthoven and the Story of Electrocardiography
Philo T. Farnsworth: The Life of Television's Forgotten Inventor
Enrico Fermi and the Nuclear Reactor
Alexander Fleming and the Story of Penicillin
Henry Ford and the Assembly Line
Robert Goddard and the Liquid Rocket Engine
Otto Hahn and the Story of Nuclear Fission
William Hewlett: Pioneer of the Computer Age
Godfrey Hounsfield and the Invention of CAT Scans
Edwin Hubble and the Theory of the Expanding Universe
Robert Jarvik and the First Artificial Heart
Willem Kolff and the Invention of the Dialysis Machine
Barbara McClintock: Pioneering Geneticist
Lise Meitner and the Atomic Age
Joseph E. Murray and the Story of the First Human Kidney Transplant
Linus Pauling and the Chemical Bond
John R. Pierce: Pioneer in Satellite Communications
Charles Richter and the Story of the Richter Scale
Sally Ride: The Story of the First American Female in Space
Edward Roberts and the Story of the Personal Computer
Wilhelm Roentgen and the Discovery of X Rays
Jonas Salk and the Polio Vaccine
Edward Teller and the Development of the Hydrogen Bomb
Selman Waksman and the Discovery of Streptomycin
Robert A. Weinberg and the Search for the Cause of Cancer
Stephen Wozniak and the Story of Apple Computer

Henry Ford and the Assembly Line

Copyright © 2004 by Mitchell Lane Publishers, Inc. All rights reserved. No part of this book may be reproduced without written permission from the publisher. Printed and bound in the United States of America.
Printing   1   2   3   4   5   6   7   8   9   10

Library of Congress Cataloging-in-Publication Data
Bankston, John, 1974
        Henry Ford and the assembly line/John Bankston.
            p. cm. — (Unlocking the secrets of science)
        Summary: Examines the life and accomplishments of Henry Ford, who among other things, is credited with inventing the assembly line, which changed not only the automotive industry but all industries.
        Includes bibliographical references and index.
        ISBN 1-58415-173-0 (Library Bound)
        1. Ford, Henry, 1863-1947—Juvenile literature. 2. Automobile industry and trade—United States—Biography—Juvenile literature. 3. Industrialists—United States—Biography—Juvenile literature. 4. Assembly-line methods—Juvenile literature. [1. Ford, Henry, 1863-1947. 2. Industrialists. 3. Automobile industry and trade—Biography. 4. Assembly-line methods.] I. Title. II. Series.
        TL140.F6 B35 2002
        338.7'6292'092—dc21   2002008324

ABOUT THE AUTHOR: Born in Boston, Massachussetts, **John Bankston** began publishing articles in newspapers and magazines while still a teenager. Since then, he has written over two hundred articles, and contributed chapters to books such as *Crimes of Passion*, and *Death Row 2000*, which have been sold in bookstores across the world. He has written more than three dozen biographies for young adults, including *Francis Crick and James Watson: Pioneers in DNA Research*, *Robert Goddard and the Liquid Rocket Engine*, and *Alexander Fleming and the Story of Penicillin* (Mitchell Lane). He has worked in Los Angeles, California as a producer, screenwriter and actor. Currently he is in pre-production on *Dancing at the Edge*, a semi-autobiographical screenplay he hopes to film in Portland, Oregon. Last year he completed his first young adult novel, *18 to Look Younger.* He currently lives in Portland, Oregon.

PUBLISHER'S NOTE: In selecting those persons to be profiled in this series, we first attempted to identify the most notable accomplishments of the 20th century in science, medicine, and technology. When we were done, we noted a serious deficiency in the inclusion of women. For the greater part of the 20th century science, medicine, and technology were male-dominated fields. In many cases, the contributions of women went unrecognized. Women have tried for years to be included in these areas, and in many cases, women worked side by side with men who took credit for their ideas and discoveries. Even as we move forward into the 21st century, we find women still sadly underrepresented. It is not an oversight, therefore, that we profiled mostly male achievers. Information simply does not exist to include a fair selection of women.

        This story is based on the author's extensive research, which he believes to be accurate. Documentation of that research can be found on p. 47.

        The internet sites referenced in this book were all active as of the date of publication. Due to the fleeting nature of some Web sites, we cannot guarantee they will all be active when you are reading this book.

Contents

Eli Whitney's best known invention was the cotton gin, a labor
saving device for separating the seeds from cotton. Although
he'd be remembered for the cotton gin, it was his development of
interchangeable parts in 1798 that has had the greatest
influence on modern manufacturing techniques. First used in the
construction of muskets, today it is used for a variety of
products, including automobiles.

Chapter 1

A New Way

The next time you go into a store, take a moment to really notice the items on the shelves. It doesn't matter what kind of store, whether it sells video games or groceries, fast-food chicken or laptop computers. You'll see a lot of variety in the products. And they are all relatively low-priced.

But this abundance of inexpensive consumer goods is a fairly recent development. Until the late 1700s, craftspeople produced nearly everything that people bought. Blacksmiths and watchmakers, glassblowers and cabinet makers were all skilled tradespeople. They usually began their careers as apprentices working for someone who was more experienced, learning the trade. Once they had the skills, they opened their own shop. Often the shop was also their home. The term "cottage industry" refers to the small houses where shopkeepers labored, lived and sold their products.

Although they often employed assistants and apprentices of their own, the items they produced took a great deal of time to craft. These products were both expensive and rare.

Few people, for example, owned more than one watch. In fact, watches were often handed down from generation to generation. The grandson of the original watch buyer might go to the watchmaker's grandson for repairs.

By the 1790s, this pattern began to change. Eli Whitney developed a machine to remove the seeds from short staple cotton. One of his new "cotton gins" could clean the same amount of cotton as fifty people. It was the first labor-saving device. Many more would follow.

Though Whitney is best known for his cotton gin, a later innovation of his became even more important to modern manufacturing. In 1798, his factory began producing muskets for the U.S. government. Previously, muskets had been assembled by one person. But Whitney pioneered the concept of interchangeable parts. He made sure that each part of the musket could be produced in identical batches. The parts then fit together interchangeably. Although developed in France, the concept first gained wide acceptance in the United States, becoming known as the "American system."

"Labor-saving devices" and "interchangeable parts." These are two cornerstones of twenty-first century manufacturing. Both gained widespread use during the Industrial Revolution. During this period, which began during the 19th century, millions of farmers and other rural workers left their homes and went to the factories.

Factories offered better paying jobs and they were in the cities. But those first factories bore little resemblance to factories today. Machines were powered by steam engines and operated by low-paid workers who had minimum skills. Some were even children. All of them worked long hours in very dangerous conditions. Injuries, even deaths, were commonplace. Assembly work was done by hand, generally on large tables where baskets of parts were brought over by other workers. It was faster than earlier methods, but it was still time-consuming.

One man changed all of this. Though he was a farmer's son, he went to the big city and worked in a factory. He wound up getting fired because he figured out a way to save time. He was a dreamer whose ambitions weren't realized until he was in his forties. He was a self-taught engineer who worked for Thomas Edison before building his own company. His fame arrived as cars became popular, but although he's famous for his automobile factory, his other contributions are even more significant.

He was the first owner of a large factory to pay workers a decent wage. He increased safety. Most important for modern manufacturing, he developed the assembly line. He changed the twentieth century, and his impact is still felt today. And he once famously said, "History is more or less bunk," meaning that studying it doesn't have any value. Yet his own history has inspired generations.

His name was Henry Ford. This is his story.

Henry Ford's dreams didn't come quickly. He worked as a repairman, a farmer, and an engineer before he built his first car. Although it took him a long time to make a living at what he loved he never gave up and he never let lack of money get in the way.

Chapter 2

Hard Times

The Ford family was starving. So were their neighbors. So, it seemed, was everyone else in Ireland. The potato blight, a fungal disease which first began spreading in 1845, soon destroyed most of the Irish potato crop. Potatoes were a staple—a main food source for Irish families like the Fords, the same way rice is a staple in many Asian countries today. When the potatoes died, so did many Irish. For the Fords there was only one way to survive: escape.

So in 1847, John Ford, his wife, his mother and seven children joined thousands of their countrymen for an ocean passage which held no promises, only risks. It was the same choice made by immigrants everywhere, from the early settlers of Jamestown, Virginia in the 1600s to Chinese stowaways hiding in twenty-first century shipping containers.

The Fords booked passage on a ship bound for Canada. The trip was cheaper than one to the United States, and with seven kids every penny was precious. Unfortunately, the inexpensive tickets had an extra cost. In 1847, when the Fords left Ireland, those ships to Canada earned a nickname: "coffin ships." The passengers were packed tightly together and carried diseases with them like so much luggage. Many died during the long trans-Atlantic crossing. One of them was John Ford's wife.

After landing, the Fords made their way to Michigan. John Ford purchased 80 acres of farmland in Greenfield Township, near Dearborn and not far from the city of Detroit. After marrying Mary Litogot, John's son William set up his own farm.

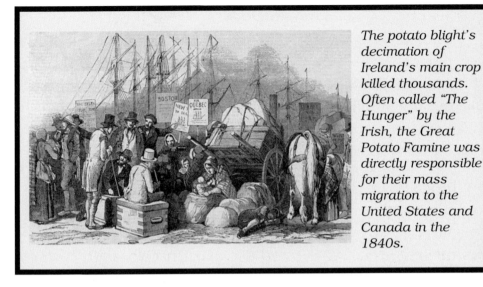

The potato blight's decimation of Ireland's main crop killed thousands. Often called "The Hunger" by the Irish, the Great Potato Famine was directly responsible for their mass migration to the United States and Canada in the 1840s.

In the early morning hours of July 30, 1863, Mary gave birth to the couple's first child, a son they named Henry. Born by candlelight on the second floor of their farmhouse, Henry entered a world which was already undergoing rapid change. To the east, the United States was engaged in one of its most bloody conflicts—the Civil War. Although the fighting between North and South had little direct impact on Michigan residents, another development in the middle of the nineteenth century did.

North America was a vast continent, and much of it was landlocked—away from oceans or cargo-carrying rivers. Railroads provided the first solution to the problems of transportation. In 1850, the United States had 9,000 miles of track. Eleven years later the figure more than tripled. Much of the backbreaking work of laying track was done by some of the over two million Irish who had immigrated to the United States.

In 1869, just a few years after Henry's birth, rails from east and west were joined in the state of Utah. It was the first transcontinental railroad and the first step in opening up travel to the average person. Every year it became a little bit easier for people to leave their home towns and go to new places. This was a process Henry accelerated as an adult. When he was born, only 20 percent of Americans lived in cities. Eighty years later more than three quarters of the population would call a city home.

Henry acquired his love for big city life early. Many of the things farmers needed could only be purchased in cities. So William and Mary made weekly shopping trips to nearby Detroit. They often brought along their young son. Henry was mesmerized and immediately fell in love with the fast-paced life. It seemed like everything interesting was going on at once.

However, back home the weight of family expectations rested heavily on Henry's shoulders. He was the son of a farmer, who in turn was the son of a farmer—all the way back as far as the Fords could trace their family line. As the oldest (Henry would eventually have five younger siblings) he was expected to take on the most responsibility. There was only one problem. Henry hated farm work. He hated the plowing, the hard labor, mostly he hated the horses. Surely there had to be a better way to move carts and equipment than with these surly beasts.

But there wasn't. "My earliest recollection," Henry would later write, "is that considering the results, there was too much work on the place. That is the way I still feel about farming."

It wasn't all work. In the evenings, the family would often play cards when the dishes were done. During the winter, the nearby river froze over and the children could go ice skating.

But the necessity for doing chores always hung over Henry's head. His complaints both angered and bewildered his father. Even away from the farm, at the tiny rural school he attended with the children of other farmers, Henry didn't do very well. He was a terrible speller and reading bored him. Only math made sense, because he had a natural gift for numbers.

But what he truly enjoyed was mechanics. He loved taking things apart. Even more important, he loved putting them back together. There was only one person in young Henry's life who seemed to understand him. That was his mother. Mary realized her son wasn't cut out for farm life. Unlike her husband, she didn't think this was a problem. She saw his other skills. Like many moms she believed her child would someday do great things. She called Henry her "born mechanic," referring to his talent at putting things together.

It was a skill others picked up on as well. His brothers and sisters tried to hide their windup toys from him. They knew that if he found the toys, he'd take them apart to see how they worked. Then one day a friend of Henry's handed him a broken watch during church. He pried it open and examined the inner works. In only a few moments he got the gears turning again.

Henry soon developed a reputation for his mechanical ability. People began bringing everything from broken watches to disabled farm equipment to the young Ford boy. Usually he could make things work again. It was a gift. Yet the arguments with his father increased. As the oldest son of a growing family, Henry was expected to act like a man. His father saw Henry's passion for putting things back together as a childish hobby. Although it might come in handy for keeping the farm equipment working, it wasn't a future.

Mary disagreed, and encouraged her son to learn as much as he could about the rapidly changing world of machines. She was his biggest champion. Despite his five siblings, she always made time for him.

In early 1876, Mary gave birth to another child. The labor was difficult, and medical care for pregnancies was poor. The baby was stillborn. A few days later, Mary passed away as well.

The loss of a parent is always tragic, but twelve-year-old Henry hadn't just lost his mother. He'd lost the only person who believed in him. The Ford family farm became a bleak place. To Henry, it was "like a watch without a mainspring," as he'd later recall.

Henry felt very alone. His father tried his best to help. Although William was also grief-stricken, the older man made sure to make time for his son, bringing him along on trips to Detroit. One such trek in the summer after his mother died changed Henry's life.

By then, steam engines powered everything from locomotives to factory equipment. They ran the small sawmills that farmers set up when they cleared the land, and the threshing machines which separated valuable grain from straw. Invented more than 150 years earlier by Thomas Newcomen and then perfected by James Watt, steam engines had become a common sight.

The principle was simple. Water was heated to boiling. The steam that was produced operated pistons which drove the machinery.

Steam engines were large and bulky. They would be loaded on horse-drawn wagons and moved from place to place. So Henry was startled as he sat beside his father on that summer afternoon. He saw someone actually driving a steam engine.

"I had seen plenty of these engines hauled around by horses," Henry would remember, "but this one had a chain that made a connection between the engine and the rear wheels of the wagon-like frame on which the boiler was mounted. The engine was placed over the boiler and one man standing on the platform shoveled coal, managed the throttle and did the steering."

Henry was fascinated. At last there was something to replace those cranky horses! The engine stopped to let the Fords' cart pass by. But Henry leaped off and asked the driver every question he could think of. Even better, the man allowed Henry to climb on board and fire the engine.

The event changed his life. Ever since that summer day, he recalled later in his life, "My great interest has been in making a machine that would travel the roads."

His days on the farm had always been difficult. Now they seemed endless. His future stretched before him like a promise, but he didn't know how he was going to make it. School was boring and at home all his father seemed interested in was convincing Henry he should be a farmer. But farmers didn't change the world. And Henry knew he was going to change the world.

The only answer was to get out, get away, get all the way to Detroit. So after helping his father bring in the harvest in the summer of 1879, Henry didn't go back to the one-room school he'd attended for eight years. Instead, he dropped out and walked several miles to Detroit.

Henry started as a mechanical apprentice at the Michigan Car Company, which manufactured railroad cars. His starting wage was $1.10 a day, pretty good wages for an apprentice. Unfortunately, less than a week into his new job, he made a tremendous mistake. In a few minutes, he solved a problem the senior employees had been trying to fix all day. His fellow workers were furious. They were sure he would cost them their jobs. So they conspired to get Henry fired. "I learned then not to tell all you know," Henry admitted later.

Henry quickly obtained an apprenticeship with the James Flower & Brothers Machine Shop. The company made many different products and had a wide variety of machines. That made it an ideal place for Henry to learn.

Henry went back to the farm the next harvest season to help out. Then he returned to Detroit and had yet another apprenticeship, this one at Detroit Dry Dock. But when it was over, Henry realized sadly there was no way he could afford to stay in Detroit. So he returned home in 1882.

William Ford welcomed his return. As far as William was concerned, his son had had his shot at boyish dreams. Now it was time to do a man's job.

In 1888, Henry Ford made a decision. He set his dreams aside and took over some land his father had given him, finally becoming a farmer. He did it all so he could marry Clara Jane Bryant.

Chapter 3

A Normal Life

But Henry hadn't given up. In his head the ideas spinning round were more dramatic than ever. He'd seen enough in Detroit to know more than ever that his future wasn't as a farmer.

Yet even at home the world was changing as new technologies arrived. William's neighbor John Gleason bought a brand new Westinghouse steam engine. Smaller and faster than previous models, it was "state of the art." Gleason planned to rent it out to local farms where it would power their equipment. There was only one problem. The new engine frightened his hired men. They refused to operate it.

Gleason already knew Henry could handle and repair steam engines better than anyone else in town. So he asked him to take on the new steam engine. Henry was nervous, but agreed to give it a try. So, just like teens today who introduce their parents to the Internet, it took a kid to show the adults how to handle the new technology.

It was the best job he'd had. Henry looked back fondly on that summer, saying, "I was paid three dollars a day and had 83 days of steady work. I traveled from farm to farm and I threshed our own and our neighbor's clover, hauled loads, cut corn stalks, ground feed, sawed wood. It was hard work."

The hard work led to a new opportunity. During his first summer running the steam engine, he met an agent from the Westinghouse company. The man was so impressed with Henry's skills that he hired the 19-year-old to be both demonstrator and repairman. It was a very responsible position, and Henry was up to the challenge. For the next several years, whenever a piece of Westinghouse equipment broke down in Southern Michigan, Henry was usually the one who solved the problem. So even though he still lived on his father's farm, he didn't do any farm work. He was either on the road for Westinghouse or tinkering in a small machine shop he set up.

When he wasn't hard at work, Henry relaxed by going to dances. At a New Year's Day dance in 1885, he met eighteen-year-old Clara Jane Bryant. Even though he was immediately interested in her, he wouldn't see her again for nearly a year. He was too busy. Henry was often gone from Dearborn, but on his travels he thought of her. Then he saw her again at another dance. This time he didn't waste his chance. Beginning in February of 1886, they began

Detroit was the city Henry had embraced as a child and moved to as an adult. Because of his influence it would become a primary center of manufacturing cars through much of the 1900s.

"courting," the very strict dating ritual which usually led to marriage. Indeed, just two months later, Henry asked Clara for her hand.

Clara said yes. Her mother said no.

Getting the mother's permission meant everything. Without it, Clara wouldn't even consider a marriage proposal. Although her mother said Clara was too young to marry Henry, he suspected another explanation: money.

His father came to the rescue. William had purchased 40 acres of land from a neighbor. The property even came with a small house. If Henry was willing to work the land and turn it into a good farm, he could have it. Henry, not wanting to lose Clara, agreed.

Henry bought a small sawmill. He not only chopped down the acres of trees on the land, but he also turned them into lumber and sold them for a profit. He used his sawmill to help his neighbors clear their land. He also installed and repaired machinery throughout the area. It was all very industrious and it definitely impressed Clara and her family.

The couple married in 1888. Henry soon built a better house on the land, relying on plans he'd developed with Clara. Before long everything about Henry's life looked almost as settled and "normal" as his father's, his grandfather's, and practically every adult male in Greenfield Township.

But there was one very important difference. Henry still had his dreams. And he wasn't about to settle for "normal."

Henry and his wife Clara are joined by their grandson, Henry Ford II on the Quadricyle built in 1896. This picture appeared in May of 1946, not long before the inventor's death.

Chapter 4

Quadricycle!

Instead of thinking about planting seeds and buying chickens, Henry thought about engines. Engines were what drove industry, and they'd fascinated him since that day over a decade before when he'd seen one being driven. Yet he knew that steam engines were an imperfect solution. They sure beat horses when it came to turning trees into lumber, but just like a barely tamed animal the machines could be dangerous and unpredictable. When he was a young teenager, Henry learned first hand just how dangerous steam can be. As an experiment, he'd plugged up the spout of a tea kettle. Then he heated the water to boiling.

The kettle exploded.

Steam engines had similar problems, and scores of people had been killed or severely injured when they blew up.

There was another problem. Steam engines required huge amounts of fuel to keep their fires burning. Even the steam engine on wheels that had excited Henry's imagination in 1876 towed a large trailer that contained wood and water. That was clearly impractical.

To solve these problems, experiments had been going on in Europe for years to replace steam engines with something safer and more efficient. Many thought the answer was the internal combustion engine.

The internal combustion engine was an entirely different concept from the steam engine. With a steam engine, the fuel is burned in a space separate from the engine. But with an internal combustion engine the fuel is burned, or combusted, inside the engine itself.

In 1876, a German engineer named Nikolaus August Otto invented the four-stroke motor. A piston was placed tightly inside a hollow cylinder. The piston was connected to a rod. The rod, in turn, was connected to a crankshaft which could run the wheels of a vehicle.

The first of the four strokes—called the intake stroke—began with the piston at the top of the cylinder. As the crankshaft turned, the piston would descend. That would suck a mixture of fuel and air into the cylinder through the intake valve.

The second, or compression, stroke was the upward movement of the piston with the intake valve closed. That would compress the air/fuel mixture. As the piston neared the top of the cylinder, a spark would be generated.

That spark created a small, controlled explosion of the compressed air/fuel mixture. Called the power or

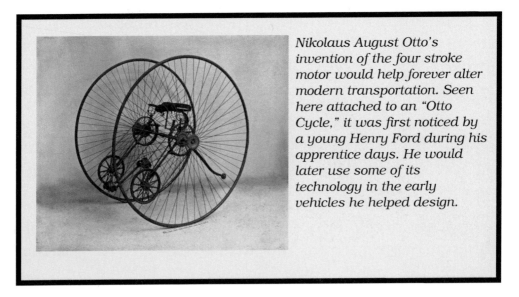

Nikolaus August Otto's invention of the four stroke motor would help forever alter modern transportation. Seen here attached to an "Otto Cycle," it was first noticed by a young Henry Ford during his apprentice days. He would later use some of its technology in the early vehicles he helped design.

combustion stroke, it would push the piston downward again.

The fourth, or exhaust, stroke was another upward movement of the piston. This time an exhaust valve opened, and the spent gases were forced out of the cylinder. When the piston reached the top of the cylinder, the sequence would begin again.

Although many different fuels were tested in running the motor—kerosene, oil, anything else that was flammable— it turned out that gasoline was the best because it burned so easily.

Henry had come across an Otto four-stroke motor when he worked for Detroit Dry Dock. Now as he puttered around his farmhouse, he thought about Otto's engine. And he thought about the men he'd read about, men in Europe who were building the first "horseless carriages," the very first cars. "Rich men's toys" are what most people called them. The vehicles were so rare that in some cities a man

Dangerous and unpredictable, steam engines were still widely used well into the 1900s. Here in 1901 loggers pose beside their "walking donkey," a steam engine used to pull down railroad tracks.

would walk ahead of them holding a red flag. The signal was to let those with horses know a car was coming.

Back in the U.S. a few hundred tinkerers and dreamers were busy building their own cars in various sheds, barns and backyards across the country. Henry knew he wanted to join their number, but not as a hobbyist. He wanted to build cars for everyone, cars that would replace those surly horses. To do that, he needed to figure out a way to make them cheaply and quickly. That was the only way that cars would stop being "rich men's toys."

He shared his dreams with Clara. One day he even sketched his idea for a "horseless carriage" and showed it to her. It was on the back of one of the sheets of organ music that Clara would play in the evenings while her husband read scientific and technical magazines. Clara's faith seemed to match his mother's. Henry would always call his supportive wife "the Believer."

But for Henry there was one major problem.

In an internal combustion engine the tiny explosions are created by the electricity generated by the spark plug. Henry didn't know how to do that. So he realized he'd have to learn everything he could about electricity to understand spark plugs, and the basic system of internal combustion engines. But there weren't any schools to teach him what he needed to know. Besides, for Henry the best school was always his work.

And the best job for someone in the 1890s who wanted to learn about electricity was at a company owned by one man: Thomas Edison. Edison was the inventor of everything from the light bulb to the motion picture projector. He made much of his money from the companies that supplied electricity to power his inventions. One of those companies was in Detroit.

The Edison Illuminating Company was eager to hire a young man with a strong background in engine repair, along with a completed mechanic's apprenticeship. Henry Ford was offered the position of night engineer, working from 6:00 p.m. to 6:00 a.m. That was prime time for a company worried about keeping the light bulbs lit. Henry would be a "troubleshooter," someone who could solve problems. He couldn't wait to get started. He'd be paid to learn about electricity, and surrounded by other mechanically minded young men. Even better, he wouldn't have to worry about farming.

Henry Ford needed to learn about spark plugs so he got a job working for the Edison Illuminating Company. The job led to a meeting with Thomas Edison, the company's founder and the developer of the motion picture projector. The two would be friends into their old age. Here Ford shakes an elderly Edison's hand as tire manufacturer Harvey Firestone looks on.

Clara was stunned. Henry expected her to pick up and leave the town she'd been born in, the place where she'd grown up. All her friends and family lived there. He wanted her to abandon their new home and settled life for a shot in the dark—an opportunity which might not even pan out.

But what could she do? She packed their things into a hay wagon and the young couple headed for the big city in September 1891. Only later would Clara admit the truth. That move nearly destroyed her.

The first night there, the young bride spent the night alone in a cramped and ugly duplex after Henry left for his new job. Nights spent by herself would become a familiar routine to Clara, and Henry tried to make her life as comfortable as possible.

Even though he worked long hours for the Edison Company, Henry continued to tinker. He set up a workbench in a basement room at the plant. He had a workshop in a small brick shed behind their house. He also involved Clara in his engine experiments, sometimes taking over part of the kitchen while she tried to prepare dinner.

On November 6, 1893, Clara gave birth to a son— Edsel. He was named for one of Henry's friends in the school he attended as a youngster. Edsel would be the Fords' only child.

On Christmas Eve that year, Henry was ready. He'd built a tiny one-cylinder gas engine out of a piece of gas pipe that he'd brought home from the electric plant and other scrap materials. The device was small enough to be mounted on a board, which he clamped to the kitchen sink to hold it steady. Then he ran a wire to the overhead light socket. That supplied the electrical current he needed for the spark.

Clara held a small oil can filled with gasoline in one hand. With the other, she could turn a small screw to regulate the amount of fuel that went into the cylinder. Then Henry turned a small wheel that was connected to the crankshaft.

It sputtered briefly but didn't start.

Henry made a minor adjustment. Again Clara poured in the gasoline using one of her funnels. Again Henry turned the wheel. Again it sputtered briefly.

But then it began running with an almost deafening roar. It worked!

His success fueled his desire to go even farther. Henry wanted to build a car.

The next month, Henry was promoted to chief engineer and his salary rose to $100 a month. He'd done well at the

Henry Ford's first car, assembled inside his garage was too wide for the doors. A tired but industrious Henry used an ax to widen the space. Here he pushes an early vehicle into the street.

company. But despite family obligations, he had as little interest in building a career at Edison as he'd had in building a farm.

Henry wanted to build cars. In his mind this wasn't a hobby, this was the future. To some people, Henry's goals might have seemed like just another fantasy, but he had a gift that marks many a dreamer's success. He was able to get other people excited about his dreams and get them involved in turning them into reality.

Everyone Henry met quickly learned about his ambition. Many of them joined his efforts. He recruited fellow Edison employee George Cato to design the ignition system. Car enthusiast Charles King gave Henry various spare parts. Henry's good friend Jim Bishop aided in the actual construction of the car. Slowly, over a three-year period, these men and others entered the Fords' shed that lay behind their duplex on Bagley Avenue and helped build his car.

In 1896, Thomas Edison was taken by the young man's dream. The two were introduced during a New York convention by Henry's boss, Alexander Dow. Dow had already told the famous inventor about this "car nut" who worked for them. He brought Henry over more as a gag than anything, thinking he'd give Edison a good laugh.

Barely pausing to take a breath, Henry excitedly outlined the way he was building his car. He was almost finished when Edison interrupted by pounding his hands on the table, rattling the dishes and Henry.

"Young man, that's the thing!" Edison exclaimed. "Your car is self-contained, no boiler, no heavy battery, no smoke or steam. Keep at it!"

The words meant more to Henry than Thomas Edison could imagine. They didn't just motivate him to keep building the car. They'd eventually motivate him to quit Edison's company.

On a rainy June night that same year, Henry was ready to test his first car. He called it a Quadricycle. It was an ugly and simple thing, little more than a horse buggy frame with four wheels taken from a bicycle. A four-horsepower gas engine was mounted behind the seat. The transmission was a rubber belt from the engine to the rear wheels. It didn't have a brake or a reverse gear.

He and his helpers had brought it into the shed piece by piece and assembled it. So it isn't too surprising that it was too big to get out the door. It was already past midnight. Henry had barely slept the past few days. He was tired and frustrated as Clara and Jim Bishop stood nearby.

Henry picked up a handy ax and began chopping at the door. Pieces of brick and plaster flew everywhere, but he didn't pause until a gaping hole replaced the too-small door.

Jim and Henry pushed the car out as Clara stood beneath an umbrella, watching in the misting rain. The moment of truth had arrived. Henry yanked on the flywheel, igniting the engine. It sputtered to life. Henry jumped into the driver's seat. Jim rode ahead on a bicycle, ready to warn any late night horses and buggies as Henry drove slowly down the street.

His first car ran. The next part of his life was speeding toward Henry Ford like a brakeless dragster.

The best way to get publicity for his cars was to show people what they could do. At first Henry Ford raced the cars himself. Yet even he was too scared to race his 999, so he hired Barney Oldfield to do it for him. Oldfield would set a new world record when he hit a speed over ninety miles per hour.

Chapter 5

A Model Company

By 1899, Henry Ford hadn't just built his first car—he'd sold it, for two hundred dollars. He was in his middle thirties with a good job, a small child and a devoted wife. But Henry's dreams required risk.

The Edison Illuminating Company was expanding, and Henry's supervisor Alexander Dow offered him a promotion to plant superintendent. The position meant both an increase in pay and responsibility. There was a catch, however. Henry would have to give up his "car hobby."

"I had to choose between my job and the automobile," Henry recalled later. Despite his family obligations, there was never a contest. Henry quit Edison.

Now it was time to get serious. It was time to build a company.

Henry founded the Detroit Automobile Company in the summer of 1899. A few rich investors put up the necessary money. Henry's job was to get a vehicle ready to be sold. He had ninety days.

Detroit Automobile's first product wasn't even a car. It was a truck. It was modeled after a horse-drawn delivery wagon. The investors hoped the vehicle would attract business buyers. Despite being given an incredible opportunity, Henry remained unfocused. The plant was more of an experiment, a chance to see the best way to build cars. Instead of an organized assembly system, parts of the vehicle would often just sit. The workers waited while Henry tinkered with a new idea.

It wasn't an ideal way to run a company. Fifteen months later, the company was out of business, and the dozen trucks Henry had managed to get built were sold for scrap. Almost broke, Henry let his father help him with renting a larger house. Meanwhile, Henry found another use for cars—racing.

On October 10, 1901, Henry competed against Alexander Winton, who had won more car races than any other man alive. Winton's car was more powerful and Henry had never raced before. In order to make the corners of the one-mile dirt race track, Henry had a friend ride on the side to keep the car from tipping over. Even so, he still had to slow down. Winton took an early lead. But Henry began catching up as he learned how to corner better. Late in the race, the engine on Winton's car broke down. Henry's car was better built and he won the race. When Henry accepted his trophy, a glass bowl, all Clara could say was, "Where will we put it?"

Henry's victory gave him more than a crystal bowl Clara had little use for. He was also supposed to win a $1,000 prize. Somehow the money disappeared. But Henry won something that money couldn't buy: good publicity. The newspapers wrote detailed accounts of the race. Their readers included another group of rich investors, and the Henry Ford Automobile Company was born. But once again, Henry clashed with the men paying the bills. He wanted to build a car the average man could afford. They wanted to build a car for the elite few.

Once again, he refused to let anyone rush him. Before long he was fired. He left with $900 and the rights to his own name. The Henry Ford Automobile Company became the Cadillac Motorcar Company. It would enjoy great success selling fairly expensive cars to those able to afford them.

Henry continued to build race cars. He believed that what he learned from building them would help him make better passenger vehicles.

He designed the 999, which had an 80 horsepower engine. It was so loud that he didn't drive it in Detroit's streets. It would scare too many people, he felt. And it scared him to think of driving it himself in a race. So he hired Barney Oldfield, a famous bicycle racer. Oldfield easily beat Winton in another race in 1902.

Two years later Henry himself drove the 999 over frozen Lake St. Clair. The ice was riddled with cracks. Every time the car hit one it threatened to spin out of control. But Henry managed to keep it upright and pointed straight ahead. He set a new world record of more than 91 miles an hour.

In the meantime, Alex Malcomson, a leading Detroit coal merchant, had agreed to help finance Henry's car company ambitions. A few other men joined him. On July 16, 1903, the Ford Motor Company was founded. Henry was chief engineer, and his experience building racing engines led to one of the fastest cars available then to consumers. The Model A would sell for $850, less than a year's average wages. That made it pricey for most workers but not unobtainable.

Still, it wasn't just Henry's design skills that would make the Model A successful. It was that he'd finally met his match. James Couzens was Malcomson's clerk, assigned to keep an eye on Henry. Couzens shared Henry's vision for a mass-produced car affordable to most people. But unlike

Henry, Couzens had his feet firmly planted on the ground. He was able to focus Henry as no one before him had. When the inventor wanted to keep adding innovations to the model, Couzens promised Henry they would be used on the next car. Couzens kept the line running—there was no shutting down while Henry tinkered.

By the end of 1904, the company was producing 1,700 vehicles a year. Every car found an eager buyer. In fact, demand was part of the problem. It was impossible to keep up. Cars were being built like bicycles—using Eli Whitney's concepts of interchangeable parts, an idea over a century old.

But cars weren't bicycles. They had many times more moving parts. As the company began developing the next model, Henry was already considering ways to speed the process of automotive assembly. Unfortunately, as the company gained financial success, Henry found himself again fighting familiar battles. Malcomson wanted to also build luxury cars, while Henry believed the company should only make cars for the average worker.

For a while, the company did both. The Model A was quickly followed by Models B, C, E, F, K, N, R and S. Malcomson and several others stepped aside in 1906, selling their interest in the company for a good profit.

In 1910, the successful Ford Motor Company, with Henry as president, moved to a spacious new factory in Highland Park. There he began producing what would be his company's most successful product. It was a car that, as Henry described, "will be constructed of the best materials, by the best men to be hired, after the simplest designs that modern engineering can devise. But it will be so low in price that no man making a good salary will be unable to own one."

The product lived up to the hype. Called the Model T, the car was the marriage of Henry's dreams, Couzens' business sense and the labor of thousands of workers. Nicknamed the "Tin Lizzie," it would change America. It could travel over unpaved roads from farm to farm, and city streets. It was the first automobile to cross the country under its own power. It was also the first car with a left-hand steering wheel so drivers could more easily check for oncoming traffic before pulling out to pass. It was simple to maintain. And—above all—it was affordable.

The first Model T cost $850, the same as the Model A. By the end of its production the Model T would cost less than $300. It was produced for nearly two decades. Over fifteen million Tin Lizzies would eventually be driven on roads across the world. Some still exist today.

The astounding success of the Model T made Henry Ford very rich. The grandson of the immigrant who crossed the Atlantic Ocean to Canada rather than the United States to save a few dollars became a multi-millionaire. He bought out the remaining investors in 1919 and the company came under family control. It would remain that way until 1956. Then it became a public corporation. Anyone could buy stock in the company.

Henry also became a close friend of Thomas Edison, his former employer, even though there was a 16-year difference in their ages. One likely reason for their friendship was that they had similar backgrounds. Both came from rural homes. Both served as apprentices at the start of their careers. Both were "self-made" men.

But none of those accomplishments would have been possible if Henry hadn't changed the way that cars were put together. The Model A, like other cars of the era, was assembled by workers bringing various parts to the car's metal frame, the chassis, which was bolted to sawhorses. But this method was incredibly inefficient.

Henry Ford often took the ideas of others, improved them, and made them his own. It's what he did when he designed his first car and it's what he did when he developed the assembly line. He took the advice of a number of men he worked with—many of whom built and tested the assembly line's prototypes, or first models. He looked at other companies, even meat-packing plants where hog and steer parts were carried by conveyor belts.

But for Henry, it was the lessons from childhood that he remembered best. As he looked over the final assemblies of the Model N, and at the workers beginning production in the Highland Factory, he saw nothing but disorder. Then he remembered the watches. Watches that young Henry disassembled and assembled, watches with gears working together. He'd build a factory like a watch.

First introduced in 1908, but not fully implemented until 1913, the assembly line relied on a series of conveyor belts to move car parts throughout the factory.

"Assembly would be easier, simpler, and faster if we moved the chassis along," former employee Charles Sorenson recalled in his book *My Forty Years With Ford*, "beginning at one end of the plant with a frame and adding the axles and wheels, then moving it past the stock room, instead of moving the stock room to the chassis."

At this early assembly line in Ford's Highland Park plant, auto bodies were sent down a ramp where they were lowered onto the chassis waiting below.

The bodies were assembled on the second floor. Then, like a roller coaster, they went down a slide to the chassises below on the first. It was, as Ford put it, "a wonderland of devices." Conveyors, pulleys and hooks all moved pieces of the car in an organized fashion where they were put together by workers standing in place as the parts moved by. By 1914, a car could be built in ninety minutes. Before that time it had taken over twelve hours.

Yet the new system had a major drawback. It might have been safer—workers no longer had to lug heavy car parts—but it was also boring. So boring, in fact, that workers began to quit in droves.

Henry quickly solved the problem. He more than doubled his workers' pay—from about $2.50 for a ten-hour day to $5.00 for an eight hour day. It was such a revolutionary idea that other car manufacturers complained. But Henry soon had his choice of workers, all of whom could easily afford the simple car they helped put together.

Edsel, Clara and Henry Ford (from left to right) in front of a chapel in Greenfield Village in Dearborn, Michigan on July 30, 1942. That day they watched a special program given by local children at the chapel.

Chapter 6

Controversial Henry

Henry, like many phenomenally successful men, sometimes believed he was capable of anything. In 1915, as World War I ravaged Europe, he and a group of pacifists traveled there hoping to end the war. The efforts of his "Peace Ship" were widely criticized, as was Henry's later resistance to World War II (although eventually Ford would manufacture many military products including bombers, trucks, and the first Jeep.)

He ran, unsuccessfully, for the United States Senate in 1918.

Henry also resisted change. When the Model T finally began to fall out of favor with the public, he refused to consider new models. For some time, as he once said, famously, "The customer can have the Model T painted any color he wants, so long as it's black." The company lost millions of dollars and thousands of customers before it eventually retooled and built newer models.

One of the most successful newer models was the Ford V-8, an affordable eight-cylinder automobile. Before its introduction in 1932, engines of that size were available in only a few very expensive makes.

Two years later, Henry received two enthusiastic letters that endorsed the performance of his new V-8 design. But he couldn't use either one to help advertise the car. That was because the letters came from two of the country's most notorious bank robbers, who used the V-8 as a getaway car. One was Clyde Barrow, who wrote that "The Ford has

Here on board his "Peace Ship," Henry hoped to discourage European leaders from involving themselves in what would be known as World War I. He failed, as he did in his quest to keep the U.S. out of World War II, a war where his company would eventually earn millions selling Jeeps and other equipment to the military.

got ever [sic] other car out there skinned and even if my business hasn't [sic] been strictly legal it don't hurt eny [sic] thing to tell you what a fine car you got in the V8." The other was John Dillinger. "You have a wonderful car," he said. "Been driving one for three weeks. It's a treat to drive one. Your slogan should be, Drive a Ford and watch the other cars fall behind you. I can make any other car take a Ford's dust."

But not even such an outstanding automobile could save them. Both men were shot dead by lawmen within a few weeks of writing their boastful letters.

Henry attracted the greatest criticism in two areas of his later life. Indeed his views have even managed to cloud the great accomplishments of his life.

Henry wrote about his anti-Semitic views during the early 1920s in a newspaper he purchased, *The Dearborn Independent.* Anti-Semitism—or hatred of Jewish people— would eventually be one of the causes of World War II. Henry wrote things like, "When there is something wrong in this country, you'll find the Jews." Yet he had a close personal friend who was a Jewish scholar. Every year he sent the man a new Model T.

Henry eventually backed away from his anti-Semitism. However, his anti-union fever lasted most of the rest of his life. Unions are organizations of workers who band together for higher wages and better working conditions. Sometimes they go on strike, walking out on a job and marching around outside the work place. Henry could never understand why his workers felt they needed a union. He already paid them better than most unionized workers and believed a union would just get in the way. The Ford factories were often subjected to strikes and other union activity. Ford employees sometimes used brutal methods to suppress them.

In 1933, the United States was in the middle of a depression, a period of high unemployment and economic uncertainty. The government developed a code of conduct that it wanted auto makers to sign. One of its conditions was that the auto makers allow unions and pay workers a certain wage.

Henry refused to sign. "If we tried to live up to it, we would have to live down to it," he said. No matter how much the government pressured him, Henry insisted that as a private business owner he should not be dictated to by the government. In 1935, the United States Supreme Court ruled the code unconstitutional. That meant it could not be enforced. In 1941, the Ford Motor Company finally signed an agreement with the United Auto Workers after a number of strikes.

But Henry wasn't all controversy. He established a hospital for his workers. And in 1936, he established the Ford Foundation for "advancing human welfare." It has given away more than eight billion dollars since its founding.

On the evening of April 7, 1947, the Rouge River, swollen with rain, flooded its banks and knocked out the power to the Dearborn house where Henry and Clara lived. Clara went around and lit candles as Henry lay in his bedroom, very sick. Just before midnight Henry Ford died. He left the world as he'd entered it, beneath the glow and flickering shadows of candlelight.

Yet the innovations he'd developed had changed the world forever.

Henry Ford's ambition and perseverance made him one of the richest and best known Michigan residents. His funeral was attended by thousands – admirers, workers, family and friends.

Henry Ford Chronology

1863	born on July 30 in Greenfield Township, Michigan
1876	mother dies; sees his first "riding" steam engine
1879	leaves the family farm for Detroit.
1882	returns to family farm after completing apprenticeship
1888	marries Clara Jane Bryant
1890	begins early experiments with "horseless carriage"
1891	employed by Edison Illuminating Company in Detroit
1893	son Edsel is born
1896	completes his first car, the Quadricycle
1899	quits job at Edison to devote his time to manufacturing cars; founds Detroit Automobile Company
1901	founds Henry Ford Company
1902	quits Henry Ford Company, which becomes Cadillac Motor Car Company
1903	Ford Motor Company is incorporated
1904	sets world speed record on frozen Lake St. Clair near Detroit
1908	introduces famous Model T
1910	opens Highland Park factory
1913	introduces first moving automobile assembly line
1914	begins paying workers $5 for an eight-hour work day (competitors pay around $2.50 for a ten-hour day)
1915	embarks on mission aboard his "Peace Ship" to end World War I in Europe
1918	runs for U.S. Senate seat in Michigan but loses
1919	acquires complete control of Ford Motor Company; son Edsel becomes president
1933	battles against unions and government requirements
1941	signs contract with United Auto Workers; develops first "Jeep"
1942	temporarily stops producing civilian cars in favor of military vehicles
1943	son Edsel dies at age 49
1947	dies on April 7

Automobile Timeline

1798	Muskets with interchangeable parts developed by Eli Whitney are first "mass produced" products in U.S.
1815	Scottish surveyor John McAdam begins improving road conditions in England with new paving method
1839	Philadelphian Charles Goodyear accidentally drops mixture of rubber, sulfur and lead on a hot stove and invents "vulcanized rubber," which will later be widely used for automobile tires
1851	Kentucky resident William Kelly and British inventor Sir Henry Bessemer both discover method of blowing air through molten iron to create steel; stronger than iron and more flexible, it will be widely used in automobile manufacturing
1876	Nikolaus August Otto invents four-stroke motor, a working internal combustion engine safer and more effective than steam engines
1885	Karl Benz builds first vehicle to utilize internal combustion engine
1886	Gottlieb Daimler builds four-wheeled carriage that uses internal combustion engine
1888	John Dunlop of Ireland develops pneumatic (air-filled) tire
1897	Ransom E. Olds forms REO Motor Car Company and produces Oldsmobiles
1902	David Dunbar Buick forms Buick Motor Company; Detroit Automobile Company is renamed Cadillac Motorcar Company after Antoine de la Mothe Cadillac, who founded Detroit in 1701
1908	Buick Motor Company President William Durant acquires Oldsmobile and Cadillac to form General Motors
1911	Durant and French racing driver Louis Chevrolet found Chevrolet Motor Company; name means "little mountain goat"
1912	Cadillac becomes first company to offer electric starters
1914	Brothers John and Horace Dodge form Dodge Motor Car Company
1918	Chevrolet joins General Motors
1924	Walter Chrysler founds Chrysler Corporation; Benz and Daimler companies merge to form Mercedes-Benz
1935	First freeway opens in Germany, where it is known as "autobahn"
1938	Volkswagen Beetle first placed into production
1942	Civilian car production halts for World War II
1943	Edsel Ford dies at age 49
1945	Henry Ford II, Edsel's son named president of Ford
1947	Henry Ford dies at age 83
1955	U.S. produces a record 9 million vehicles
1963	Front seat belts become standard on all vehicles
1970	Lee Iococca named president of Ford
1978	Iococca leaves Ford; becomes president of Chrysler
1987	Henry Ford II dies
2003	Ford begins 18-month trial of their THINK CITY electric car with top speed of 56 mph.

For Further Reading

For Young Adults:

Aird, Hazel B. *Henry Ford: Young Man with Ideas.* New York: Aladdin Books, 1986.

Barry, James P. *Henry Ford and Mass Production.* New York: Franklin Watts, Inc., 1973.

Corrick, James A. *The Industrial Revolution.* San Diego, CA: Lucent Books, Inc., 1998.

Culligan, Judy (editor). *MacMillan Profiles: Scientists and Inventors.* New York: Simon and Schuster, 1998.

Gourley, Catherine. *Wheels of Time: A Biography of Henry Ford.* Brookfield, CT: Millbrook Press, 1997.

Malam, John. *Henry Ford.* Chicago: Heinemann Library, Reed Educational, 2001.

Middleton, Haydn. *What's Their Story? Henry Ford.* London: Oxford University Press, 1997.

Mitchell, Barbara. *We'll Race You, Henry: A Story About Henry Ford.* Minneapolis, MN: Carolrhoda Books, 1986.

Weitzman, David. *Model T: How Henry Ford Built a Legend.* New York: Crown Publications, 2002.

On the Web:

http://www.bbc.co.uk/cgi-bin/history

http://www.top-biography.com

http://www.k-wz.de/vmotor/v_omotore.html

http://www.howstuffworks.com/steam

http://www.hykos.com/hford/

http://www.infoplease.com

http://www.ford.com/en/ourCompany/Centennial

Works Consulted:

Bryan, Ford R. *Beyond the Model T: The Other Ventures of Henry Ford.* Detroit: Wayne State University Press. 1997.

Donnelly, Jr., James S. *The Great Irish Potato Famine.* Gloucester, UK: Sutton Publishing, 2001.

Ford, Henry. *Today and Tomorrow.* New York: Productivity, reprinted 1986.

Sorenson, Charles E. *My Forty Years With Ford.* New York: W.W. Norton and Company, Inc., 1956.

Lewis, L. David. *The Public Image of Henry Ford,* Detroit: Wayne State University Press, 1976.

Werling, Donn Paul. *Henry Ford: A Hearthside Perspective.* Society of Automotive Engineers, 2000.

Glossary

· ·

apprentice - person who works for low wages so he/she can be trained by an experienced worker

assembly line - method where parts are assembled in a certain order by workers

automation - assembly of products using machines

chassis - rectangular steel frame that holds body and engine of an automobile

conveyor belt - thick belt which automatically moves items to workers

interchangeable parts - items produced identically so they can be used the same way

internal combustion engine - motor in which power is generated by the burning of fuel inside it

labor-saving device - device which makes a job faster or easier

musket - early form of the rifle

pacifist - person who believes in avoiding war and fighting

Index

· ·